Scuttlebutt Investor

Mariusz Skonieczny

Investment Publishing

Mariusz Skonieczny/Investment Publishing
1202 Far Pond Cir
Mishawaka, IN 46544
www.classicvalueinvestors.com

Ordering Information:
Quantity sales. Special discounts are available on quantity purchases by corporations, associations, and others. For details, contact the "Special Sales Department" at the address above.

Scuttlebutt Investor/ Mariusz Skonieczny. —1st ed.
ISBN 978-0-9848490-4-8

Table of Contents

Introduction

Introduction

A round July 2012, discount flooring retailer Lumber Liquidators was on a tear. Over the past quarter, net sales had increased 19.9 percent, net income had increased 130.4 percent, and gross profit margins matched the record set the previous quarter at 37.3 percent. These results boosted the stock price to $44 per share, and in November 2013, it would reach its all-time high of nearly $120 per share. It seemed like the perfect investment.

But during that same 17-month timeframe, in spite of the company turning out record profits, a very different story would emerge. The company would not only face accusations of selling toxic flooring, but its offices and one store location would be raided by federal authorities. They were looking for evidence that the company was selling flooring made from illegally harvested timber. In February

2016, the price of the stock would hit a low of nearly $10 per share.

As investors, there are some obvious questions for us to ask. Were these allegations true? Was this how the company was achieving such great results? Would the company survive these scandals, and if so, would it be able to return to a high level of profitability? Before we talk about how to answer these questions, let me give you some more background on what happened.

In June 2013, Los Angeles-based investor Xuhua Zhou wrote an article for SeekingAlpha.com about his research on the company. He was wondering how the company's gross profit margins, then over 40 percent, could be so high. For years, they had been at 33-35 percent, in line with those of competitors Home Depot and Lowe's. But around 2012, they started to increase. In his article, Zhou also pointed out that he had read online reviews. He found two where customers were complaining of irritated eyes, respiratory stress, headaches, skin rashes, and burning throats.

Laminate and engineered wood flooring are usually constructed with resin that contains formaldehyde. It is a known carcinogen that can also cause eye, nose, and throat irritation, and respiratory ailments, among other reactions. Excessive levels are considered unsafe.

Zhou purchased some Lumber Liquidators' flooring and sent samples to two labs for testing. The results of those tests showed that the samples exceeded the limits set by the California Air Resources Board (CARB). In his article, he speculated on the possible repercussions for the company—product recalls, legal fees, and regulatory fines. The television program *60 Minutes* picked up the story and, after doing an undercover investigation in China, ran an episode about it in March 2015. Customers were scared and the share price went from $51.86 to $38.26 overnight.

The raid came in September 2013 after a multi-year undercover investigation by a nonprofit organization called the Environmental Investigation Agency (EIA). Investigators had been tracking illegally harvested timber from old-growth forests in the Russian Far East, home to the world's last 450 Siberian tigers and some of the less than 50 remaining Amur leopards. They followed the wood through Chinese factories and warehouses all the way to store showrooms. One particular Chinese-owned wood flooring company was found to be the most closely linked to the illegal logging, and Lumber Liquidators was found to be its largest customer. Importing illegally harvested timber into the United States is prohibited by the Lacey Act. The EIA passed its findings on to federal authorities before the raid. Afterwards, it published a 64-page report, *Liquidating the Forests*, about its investigation.

The fallout from these two situations was $13.15 million in penalties for the illegally harvested wood, a $2.5 million settlement with CARB, hundreds of lawsuits, and much more. The company was required to forfeit millions of dollars worth of assets, implement an environmental compliance plan, and conduct a series of independent audits. While the fines were not a huge burden for a company of this size, the end of these two practices was expected to present more of a challenge.

I wanted to share this story with you because it is a great example of a situation where the scuttlebutt method, the topic of this book, can really open up a whole new world of information. The term "scuttlebutt" became popular in value investing circles after Philip Fisher wrote about it in his 1958 book, *Common Stocks and Uncommon Profits*. He advised readers to speak with the management, customers, suppliers, and employees of a company in order to learn more about it.

In his book, Fisher told how his professor in graduate school, which he attended in the late 1920s, would take the students on company visits once a week. After touring the facility, they would sit down together while he grilled the management. This gave him a perspective on investment research that was different from the norm.

To research a stock, most investors just read reports written by analysts, or articles on Yahoo Finance or CNBC. They may listen to conference calls and study the information released by the company including annual reports, quarterly updates, and press releases. However, this type of research will only show you part of the story.

Ever since I started investing, I have used the scuttlebutt method. To illustrate how it could be used in this case, I called several flooring professionals—installers, inspectors, and independent flooring retailers. Some had worked with the company, some had not. Some had been hired by customers to install or inspect floors they had purchased from Lumber Liquidators. What they told me gave me a completely different perspective, and they answered questions I didn't even know I had. Was the formaldehyde issue a big deal? Not really. It's an old story and many products used to contain high levels of formaldehyde. Over time, manufacturers reduced those levels. And many companies in a variety of industries have survived similar situations.

After the *60 Minutes* episode, there was a rush of customers calling to ask for inspections, but that died down within days. Also, none of the testing done by the professionals I interviewed had resulted in violations of CARB standards. That may have been because formaldehyde breaks down in the air.

One installer compared it to painting, installing carpet, caulking, or putting in tile. It is common knowledge that adequate ventilation is required for all of these activities.

Formaldehyde is a naturally occurring chemical that is found in very small amounts in our bodies, the air we breathe, food, and many everyday products, according to the US Department of Health and Human Services' Agency for Toxic Substances and Disease Registry. It breaks down in the air, dissolves easily in water, and is quickly absorbed and broken down once it enters your body. Whether it is dangerous depends on how much, how long, and how you come in contact with it.

Furthermore, the professionals I spoke with told me that other wood flooring companies have had similar issues with their products. They said that manufacturers in China make the same product for a lot of different retailers and label it with the name of whoever buys it. They also told me that most of the wood flooring sold in the US is made in China.

Would the company go out of business? None of them thought it was likely. Customers want to save money and Lumber Liquidators offers deals, they said. Most were of the opinion that the company has a reputation for selling a low-end product. However, a few people I spoke with were quick to point out that, like other flooring retailers, the company sells "good, better, and best" products to try to satisfy all levels of the market. They said the company does have some good products, but they cost more.

Others put the blame on customers that buy a $2 per square foot product and expect it to perform like a high-end product. Some said they refused to install Lumber Liquidators' floors. Others told me that they would only agree to install the product if they could see it first because sometimes the quality was fine and other times it was not. One told me that some of the product sold by the company is so thin that it leaves no room for error. The subfloor and the installation must be perfect.

I would never have seen another side to the story if I did not talk to people who know the wood flooring business. The reason I am telling you this is to drive home the point that you will never see an accurate picture of a company unless you do deep research and go after sources that are not widely used. If you are not willing to do this, then you had better hold a widely diversified portfolio which will insulate you from blowups. Unfortunately, if you choose to go this route, it is unlikely you will achieve high returns.

Anybody can read the company's website, the management's biographical descriptions, and the SEC filings. The problem is that these sources are designed to portray the company in the best light possible. They are proofread by editors and reviewed by lawyers in order to make sure investors get the best impression.

Through traditional sources, you are never going to find out whether the CEO lives large, abuses his employees, or cooks the books. Only scuttlebutt research can reveal that.

The word scuttlebutt originally referred to a barrel used to store drinking water on sailing ships. "Butt" referred to the barrel and "scuttle" meant to chop or drill a hole as for tapping a cask. Sailors would gather around the scuttlebutt to drink water, and as they did, they exchanged gossip, just the way people do today around water coolers in offices. Eventually, the term scuttlebutt came to refer not just to the barrel, but also to the rumors and gossip.

Being a scuttlebutt investor means trying to create "gossip" between yourself and parties that have had intimate relationships with the business you are studying. Obviously, you can't arrange for the managers, customers, suppliers, or employees to gather around a water cooler with you, but you can contact them individually to learn information about the particular business that you would never be able to uncover just by reading annual reports and press releases put out by the company.

CHAPTER 1

Due Diligence

Due Diligence

As a scuttlebutt investor, you are trying to learn about a business from people who have had close interactions with it. However, this does not mean that scuttlebutt research replaces the due diligence process. Scuttlebutt is only part of your due diligence. Before you interview a company's managers, clients, or competitors, you should have already acquired basic knowledge about its business. If you don't know anything about the business and its industry then you won't know how to ask proper questions and interpret the answers you are given.

This is not a book about due diligence. I wrote a separate book dedicated specifically to this subject. Also, I published a DVD on how to conduct due diligence. For this reason, I am not going to cover this topic in detail here, but you should at least complete the following steps before proceeding with the scuttlebutt portion of your research.

- Read the company's annual report or Form 10-K
- Check out the company's website
- View the investor presentation
- Learn about the products or services
- Study the financial statements
- Read the proxy statement
- Read up on the industry (through the Internet or books)
- Search for any interviews with the management

After you have finished these steps, you will have a basic understanding of the company and its industry. Because of this knowledge, you will be able to have intelligent conversations with people that will help you understand the business even better. Also, you will be able to form follow-up questions based on responses from previous questions. If you have to ask "What do you do?" to the management, you are wasting their time.

In this book, I start with the current management, and then discuss the customers, suppliers, and other sources. In reality, however, you will end up jumping from one category to another and following leads generated during your conversations. Interviewing the management first gives you ammunition and conversation material for when you talk with other sources, such as employees, clients, and competitors.

CHAPTER 2

Management

Management

Interviewing the management is the first step of scuttlebutt research. The goal is to develop a deeper understanding of the business and its strategy. Yes, you already read the annual report, but there is a lot more to learn. Also, you will ask the management some of the same questions you will ask clients and competitors. If the clients' responses are different from the management's responses, then someone is lying. That alone is worth a lot.

I almost always talk with the current management. However, I'm also aware that they won't tell me the dirt that I need to know. But I establish relationships with them because someday, they might leave, and they may be much more forthcoming. For example, I once visited a company that had just hired a new CEO to turn it around. While I was there, I had the opportunity to meet him and invite him for lunch. I also interviewed him and posted a written transcript of it on my website, which gave the company some visibility. In other words, I had made a good contact. Then, all of a sudden, he resigned. This time, when I contacted him, he really told me the ins and outs of the company. He did not hold back. As an investor, I want to know the whole story, and sometimes, it takes a long time to uncover it.

You can locate the members of the management team from the company's website or from its filings of Form 10-K, which is the company's annual report as submitted to the US Securities and Exchange Commission (SEC). If you are dealing with a small company, you will likely be able to reach the management. However, if you are dealing with a blue-chip company, then you have practically zero chance of being able to talk with the management, unless, of course, you are a big shareholder. With big companies, you will have to interview someone from the investor relations department. Either way, here are some questions that you should ask:

Why do clients buy from you? What kind of problems do you solve through your offerings?

You need to have a crystal clear understanding of why clients buy from your subject company. Without this, there is no way to figure out whether they will continue doing business with the company.

Do your clients' tastes and demands change from year to year? If so, how do you address that?

It is best when your product or service satisfies clients year after year without requiring much new development. For example, chewing gum companies can keep selling the same product year after year. This is a great business. However, if the clients' demands do change, it is not the end of the world. What is the end of the world is when the company fails to innovate in order to keep up with those changes.

Could you describe your research and development efforts? How do you come up with new products? What is your hiring process for R&D employees? What is the product development cycle? Do you have any products in the pipeline right now?

In many industries, it is the new and improved products that generate the revenues. Therefore, you should spend some time understanding this department. Also, you should compare your company's efforts to what its competitors are doing. This is why you will ask the competitors the same questions about their research and development departments.

Is the market big enough for new products or do you have to steal customers from competitors?

Public companies are required to grow. Wall Street is addicted to growth. Consequently, companies work hard to generate that growth through geographic expansion or new product development. However, if the market is already saturated and there is no more room for growth, then what is the point? You have to figure out whether what the company is pursuing has a promising future.

Could you describe your sales force? How do you reach clients? How do you compensate your salespeople? How do you train them? Where do you get your salespeople from? How do you measure the effectiveness of your marketing dollars?

I have seen countless entrepreneurs fail because the cost of acquiring clients was higher than the gross profit. This is a big deal. Your subject company must have a sales team that is able to sell the product or service in a way that generates profits. With established companies, you can look at the income or cash flow statements and see whether profit is being generated. If it is, then the company is doing something right. However, a competitor might have higher sales or better margins, which could be caused by a superior sales force.

Different businesses sell differently. You are not going to sell ice cream the same way you sell insurance. So, I can't give you a formula for how to analyze the quality of a sales team. It depends on the industry. You have to take it upon yourself to learn what successful businesses do in particular industries to successfully sell their products and services. First, you learn from the company about its sales operations, and then you compare your findings to how its competitors handle sales.

Are your clients one-time customers or are they repeat customers?

You are trying to figure out whether the business has any recurring revenues. Getting new clients is expensive while selling to existing customers is cheap. Ideally, you want the customers that keep coming back.

What are your clients' switching costs?

Sticky clients, meaning clients that are loyal, are preferable. It is great when clients find it difficult to switch from your subject company to a competitor.

For example, if your subject company is a website hosting provider, then the client is unlikely to switch. It is very painful to move a website from one hosting provider to another. It is easier to stay even if the price goes up.

How do you set the price for your product or service? Is it negotiated?

You want to figure out who has the pricing power. If your subject company is able to set the price without losing the client, then it most likely has the pricing power. However, if it has to keep lowering the price in order to keep the customer, then the customer is the one with the pricing power.

How do you maintain or improve margins?

Margins can be maintained or improved by controlling either the sales price or the costs. The ideal situation is when the subject company can raise prices without losing customers or lower expenses without losing employees and suppliers. It is all about who has more bargaining power.

If your subject company sells a product or service in a competitive industry, it is unlikely that it has much pricing power. Likewise, if it has limited choice in terms of suppliers when it comes to purchasing materials, it faces the same situation. In this case, the company might have to build economies of scale in order to maintain or improve margins.

How will you finance future growth?

The preferable answer to this question is through cash flow, but this is not always possible. If the company's growth prospects are bright, financing it with equity or debt might make sense.

Who are your closest competitors?

You can find this out yourself by reading filings of Form 10-K, but maybe you will learn about other competitors that are not listed there. This question also opens up the conversation about competitors in general.

Who are your toughest competitors?

If your subject company tells you that Company X is its toughest competitor, but when you ask Company X the same question and Company X does not even mention your subject company, then Company X is not even threatened by your company. Now, you know who is stronger.

How does your company compare to its competitors?

Let the CEO or investor relations representative tell you how great your subject company is in relation to its competitors. After you complete your scuttlebutt research, you will have a strong sense of whether the management's view is accurate or delusional.

What are the most important competitive factors to win a client?

During the scuttlebutt process, you want to learn about what is important to clients. Is it the price, quality, customer service, or dependability? Then, you can see where your company stands. Not all competitors are equal. Some focus on great customer service while others only care about being the cheapest.

Who are your suppliers?

Later on in the scuttlebutt process, you will contact the company's suppliers. You may be able to identify some of them on your own, but this is your chance to learn about some you may have missed.

Are there a lot of suppliers that you can choose from?

It is usually better if your subject company has plenty of choice in terms of suppliers. This protects the company from getting taken advantage of by a supplier who would overcharge for a product or service. Think of Walmart. With plenty of suppliers to choose from, Walmart has pricing power and takes advantage of its suppliers. As an investor, you don't want to be invested in Walmart's suppliers because you know Walmart will never allow them to be really profitable.

How difficult would it be to switch suppliers?

When it comes to clients, it is better when they face switching costs going from your subject company to a competitor, but when it comes to suppliers, it is better when your subject company's switching costs are minimal.

What kind of problems does your industry face today? What kind of problems do you anticipate for the industry in the future and how are you preparing for them?

Business is all about solving problems for others. Your managers should be well aware of the problems that their clients face so that they can be the ones to provide the solutions that will win their business. Here's an example. If you have been to a car dealership and seen their computer screens, you know that the software they have looks like the old DOS system. That's because it was built before Windows came out. It's hard to believe that any industry is still using such outdated technology. The suppliers of this software are complacent and have left the door wide open for a company called Quorum Dealer Management Systems to offer something new.

Not only does Quorum's software provide a comprehensive solution that automates, integrates, and streamlines every department within the dealership, it also allows them to communicate with customers via text and e-mail. With this software, mechanics can text the customers about additional repairs needed and receive feedback quickly, thereby increasing the chance to generate more revenue. Suppliers that don't adapt to customers' changing needs will disappear.

SUMMARY

Some investors say they never talk to the management because they do not want to be influenced by them. They say they let the numbers do the talking. However, there is a great deal of information that they miss out on. Being a scuttlebutt investor gives you an edge over those who are afraid to pick up the phone. Because you will also talk with customers, suppliers, and employees, you will not be easily swayed by the management's charisma. Actually, you will be able to catch them in a lie if you ask the same question to different groups of people.

Customers

Customers

T here is one factor that is more important than any other when it comes to making a business a success—having customers. If you do not have customers, you do not have a business. However, just because a business has customers today does not mean it will have them tomorrow. The reason why customers buy is because a company's products or services solve their problems and satisfy their needs. The moment that they are no longer satisfied, they will leave to find someone else.

At one point, I was interested in KSW Mechanical Services, a company that furnishes and installs heating, ventilation, and air conditioning systems for commercial properties in New York City. It was eventually bought out, but at that time, it was public. The stock price was extremely cheap in relation to its assets. It was literally trading at cash in the bank, but at the same time, it was profitable. I was impressed by its financial performance, but I was concerned whether its revenues were sustainable. I knew that the HVAC supply and installation business was fragmented—there aren't really any major players—and I didn't see any competitive advantage.

To find out how sustainable its business was, I called several of its current and former customers and asked them why they chose KSW Mechanical. Their responses were unanimous. They all loved working with the company. One client said, "They come in and do their job. They do not complain. You don't even know that they are there on the site." I was told that KSW stays on budget and finishes on time. I asked another client how KSW Mechanical manages to get work on so many different projects, and his response was "The CEO knows everybody, including your mother." When I asked former customers why they didn't work with them anymore, I was told that if they had another project that required that kind of work, then they would absolutely hire them again. As you can see, this kind of feedback was invaluable.

Talking to KSW's customers made me realize that the commercial market is different from the residential market, which is what I was familiar with—there are only a few players that matter, and KSW is one of them. The CEO's connections are key to staying on top and the feedback I received showed me that the company did have a competitive advantage.

As a scuttlebutt investor, you must learn from the customers why they are doing business with the company in question. They could have chosen another company to work with—why did they choose yours? You have to put yourself in their shoes and act as if you were running their business. Only then will you be able to get a sense of how important it is for them to do business with the company you are studying.

WHO ARE THE CUSTOMERS?

In certain instances, it is easy to pinpoint who the customers are. For example, everybody knows what kind of customers Walmart has. If you shop there, you see them, you rub elbows with them, and you get stuck behind them when you are trying to get through the store. However, in other instances, it is not obvious who the customers are. You need help.

Publicly traded companies are required to file various documents with the SEC. Form 10-K is just one of them. Within that document, companies explain the nature of their business and their strategy to investors and describe who their customers are. If you are lucky, they will actually list names instead of giving just a general description.

For example, CoStar Group is a company that provides commercial real estate information, such as property sales and rental information. Within its Form 10-K filing, the company says that it provides services to owners, developers, landlords, property managers, financial institutions, retailers, vendors, appraisers, investment banks, government agencies, and other parties involved in commercial real estate. Then, it provides a sample list of individual clients.

Brokers

Avison Young
Binswanger
BNP Paribas — U.K.
CB Richard Ellis
CB Richard Ellis — U.K.
Charles Dunn Company
Coldwell Banker Commercial NRT
Colliers
Colliers International UK — U.K.
CRESA
Cushman & Wakefield
Cushman & Wakefield — U.K.
DAUM Commercial Real Estate Services
Drivers Jonas Deloitte — U.K.
DTZ, a UGL company
Gerald Eve — U.K.
GVA Grimley — U.K.
HFF
Jones Lang LaSalle
Jones Lang LaSalle — U.K.
Kidder Mathews
Knight Frank LLP — U.K.
Lambert Smith Hampton — U.K.
Lee & Associates
Marcus & Millichap
Mohr Partners
Montagu Evans — U.K.
NAI Global
Newmark Grubb Knight Frank
Re/Max
Savills Commercial — U.K.
Savills Studley
Sperry Van Ness
Transwestern
USI Real Estate Brokerage Services
Voit Real Estate Services
Weichert Commercial Brokerage

Owners, Developers

Europa Capital Partners — U.K.
Hines
Industrial Developments
LNR Property Corp
Shorenstein Properties, LLC
Tishman Speyer

Retailers

7-Eleven
Carter's
Dollar General Corporation
Jos. A Bank
Massage Envy
Petco
Rent-A-Center
Sony
Spencer Gifts LLC
Walgreens

Appraisers, Accountants

Deloitte
Integra
KPMG
Marvin F. Poer
Price Waterhouse Coopers
Ryan LLC

As you can see on the list, the company provides its services to clients such as CB Richard Ellis (CBRE Group), Walgreens, and Deloitte.

Another way of getting a list of clients is to look through companies' investor presentations, which are usually available under the investor relations sections of their websites. For example, Energold Drilling, which is in the business of providing drilling services to mining, oil and gas, water, and geotechnical clients, provides the following client list in its investor presentation.

HOW TO LOCATE THE RIGHT PERSON

Once you have a partial list of customers that do business with the company you are studying, then it is time to contact them. The next step is to find the right person within the client company who actually uses the product or service. If you simply called Walgreens to ask about CoStar's services, the person on the other end of the line would not know what you are talking about. In this example, you would have to find a person in the commercial real estate department that is familiar with CoStar's services.

When I call a client company, I usually ask to speak with a person that is either using the service or is in charge of paying for the service. When asked why I want to speak with such a person, I tell them that I am trying to get a reference on a particular company's product or service and that the best contact is a customer that is actually using it. With smaller companies, this task is easy because most of the time, you can make just one phone call and get to the right person.

You can also search LinkedIn for the customer's employees. By scanning through their titles and resumes, you should be able to locate individuals that can help you or point you to the right person.

Obviously, you can also ask the subject company that you are studying for specific people that you can contact to obtain references. Just know that you will only be given names of customers that are satisfied. You will never be given names of angry clients.

WHAT TO ASK THEM

The following are some of the questions that you should ask:

Are you satisfied with the product or service?

If the clients are still doing business with your company, then they are most likely satisfied; otherwise, they would not be paying money. However, if, during your conversation with them, you sense any dissatisfaction with the product or service, then their days as clients may be numbered. Customer satisfaction may be the best indicator of how likely customers are to make more purchases in the future, according to *Marketing Metrics: The Definitive Guide to Measuring Marketing Performance*, by Paul W. Farris, et al. Thus, while sales or market share are good ways to measure a company's current performance, customer satisfaction is a way to gauge the company's future performance.

How long have you been a customer?

Longevity is a good thing because it costs money to get new clients. If you come across a lot of clients that have been with the company for a long time, this is a good sign. But if you cannot find any relatively new clients, this might not be good either because it tells you that the subject company might not be growing anymore.

What kind of problems does the product or service solve for you?

This is vital. You have to understand the kind of problems that the product or service solves. I cannot overemphasize this. For example, Essex Rental, provides cranes for construction projects. Without them, construction cannot proceed. The product is absolutely critical. Another example of a company that is very much needed by its customers is CoStar Group, which I mentioned before. Commercial real estate appraisers cannot function without the service, because it provides them with access to commercial real estate sales and rental data. Yes, in theory, this data could be reproduced in-house, but it would be prohibitively expensive. Also, it would take the appraisers three months to write an appraisal report versus three to five days with the help of CoStar.

Are there any other companies that you could use instead of the subject company?

It is the best when the client of your company desperately needs to use the product or service. However, this does not mean that the client has to buy from your company. Yes, the cranes on construction projects are critical, but there are plenty of companies that provide rental services. Consequently, Essex Rental cannot ever charge high prices or it will lose customers. CoStar, on the other hand, can charge almost whatever price it wants and customers cannot leave because there are no other companies that come even close to CoStar. Lack of competition is great for the provider and not so great for the consumer.

Why aren't you using other companies?

You can gain a great deal of insight into the competitive landscape of the industry by asking this question. If the client answers that it could use other companies without a problem, then you know that the subject company does not possess anything special, and the moment something goes wrong, the client may switch to a competitor.

How easy would it be to switch to a competitor?

Think about some of the products and services that you use, like bank accounts. It would be a huge inconvenience to switch from one bank to another. You would need new checks, online passwords, and automatic payments. This is a huge headache, especially when the new bank does not offer you anything different. When asking about switching costs, find out what the kind of hassles that the client would have to go through to make the switch happen. Would it require new training, equipment, lawyers, or penalty fees? Or would it be as simple as making a telephone call?

Could you reproduce the same product or service in-house?

Sometimes your biggest competitor is your client. Instead of outsourcing a project to you or your company, the client may choose to do it in-house. Only if it is much too expensive to do it in-house or if the company lacks the technological know-how to do it can you win their business.

Is the price tag significant to you?

If the price is insignificant, then it is unlikely that the client will try to shop around for a competitor with a cheaper price. In this case, your company might be able to raise prices without negative consequences. For example, Stericycle is a company that provides medical waste disposal for doctors, hospitals, and pharmacies. For its clients, the price tag for these services is insignificant in relation to other expenses that they face, so Stericycle is able to increase its prices year after year without losing business.

Is the price you are paying going up, down, or remaining stable from year to year?

The answer to this question might reveal who has the pricing power. Remember the example I gave earlier about Walmart. If Walmart is one of your company's clients, then you know that Walmart is the one with the pricing power. Walmart will not let its suppliers increase prices. Instead, it forces them to cut, cut, and cut. If they don't, Walmart will replace them with someone else who delivers cheaper products. From your point of view, you obviously would like your company to be the dominant player and have bargaining power over the client. If your company has to lower prices every year to keep the client, then this is not a good sign.

Can you negotiate on price?

This is a similar question that can reveal who has more bargaining power. Is the client able to negotiate with your company or do they have to take it or leave it? The stronger player usually dictates the prices and the weaker player has to accept it or be denied the product or service.

POTENTIAL CUSTOMERS

You can learn so much from your company's clients. However, if you only communicate with existing clients, you might end up with a biased picture. Existing clients are the ones who are currently using the product or service, and therefore, they are most likely satisfied. Also, they are biased toward the suppliers that they use. It is understandable because they are paying them money so, psychologically they tend to have positive feelings towards them. Therefore, you need to seek input from the customers of your competitors, who are potential clients of your company, in order to hear from people that are not emotionally invested in your subject company.

You will locate them the same way you locate clients for your subject company. Read the competitors' 10-K filings and investor presentations and look for client lists. How to locate competitors will be covered later in this book.

The following are some of the questions that you should ask:

- *Why do you do business with the competing company?*
- *What type of determining factors do you consider when choosing a supplier for your products or services?*
- *Have you ever worked with any other companies?*
- *Have you ever worked with the subject company?*
- *How do the various suppliers differ from each other?*
- *Do you know of anyone that used to work with the subject company but is no longer a client?*

FORMER CUSTOMERS

Talking with former customers can be really help you understand your subject company. However, locating them is a bit tricky. You have to put your detective hat on. Here are some ways to find them.

Remember how I told you to read filings of Form 10-K to find client lists? Go back 10 years and look at every client list from each 10-K filing and compare the clients. If a client was on the list eight years ago but is no longer listed, then this might be a former client.

Ask existing and potential clients if they know of any former clients. Ask competitors the same question. They might be the ones that stole a client away. Ask former employees of the subject company. Since they are not working with the company anymore, they might feel safe giving you the name.

Once you have a list of former customers, ask them the following questions:

Why are you no longer a client of the subject company?

Figure out whether the client left because someone else offered a better price or because the client's needs were no longer being met. It's also possible that a competitor came up with a better solution or the nature of the client's business changed.

What is different about the current supplier that is better than your former supplier?

The answer to this question will help you understand how competitive your company's products or services are in comparison to competing products. Also, you will be hearing it straight from someone who tried more than one company.

Do you know of other companies that switched to different suppliers?

This question will help you build a list of former customers. People in the industry pay attention to what other players are doing. This particular client might have switched because of a referral from someone else.

Is it difficult to switch?

You already asked this question, but this time you are asking it to someone who already switched, which means the switching costs have already been incurred. This is your chance to find out how difficult it truly is to switch. Also, find out if the switch was worth it. Maybe you can ask a follow-up question about whether this former client would switch again if the same opportunity presented itself.

Are there any circumstances under which you would consider going back to the subject company?

The answer to this question should tell you the factors that are important for clients in choosing their suppliers. For some products or services, it could be the price, quality of work, customer service, delivery speed, or provider's infrastructure.

SUMMARY

Forming an accurate picture of why some customers do business with your company and why others do not is the most important step. The idea behind this is to determine how stable and reliable the revenues are. Without that, how can you make any sort of estimates about the value of the company? The bottom line is dependent on the top line. Yes, the business has to manage its expenses properly, motivate its employees, and pay its suppliers on time, but without reliable revenues, none of that matters. You can be the best employer in the world, but if you can't satisfy your clients, you will go under. Learn why people are doing business with your company now, and this will help you project whether they will continue doing business with the company in the future.

Suppliers

CHAPTER 4

Suppliers

Suppliers affect whether a company can reliably provide its end products or services on time and at reasonable prices. Suppliers that offer the latest, most advanced products and services and have well-trained employees who can help your company effectively use those products and services can help your company be as competitive as possible.

A supplier who is flexible, adaptable, and easy to work with can help a company improve its existing products and services or even develop new ones. You want your company to choose suppliers that allow your company to visit its facilities, talk with its workers, and quiz its managers. Instead of an adversarial relationship where your company tries to bully its suppliers into offering unrealistically low prices or making other unfair concessions, a positive relationship allows your company and its suppliers to work together to control costs.

Suppliers can be manufacturers or wholesale distributors. They may provide raw materials for your company to manufacture a finished product, or they may provide finished products for resale. They are the only ones who can tell you what it is like to work with your company as a customer. Seek out current suppliers, wannabe suppliers, and former suppliers in order to see your subject company from different perspectives.

CURRENT SUPPLIERS

When public companies describe their businesses in their 10-K filings, they talk about the type of supplies that they need for their finished product or service. Sometimes, they list specific suppliers. For example, Mitcham Industries is in the business of leasing seismic equipment for the oil and gas industry. In their 10-K filing for fiscal year 2015, the company says, "From 1996 through fiscal 2014, we had a series of supply agreements with Sercel covering a variety of products." Sercel is a leading designer and manufacturer of seismic equipment.

In Mitcham's case, it was easy to locate this supplier because the company specifically named it. In other cases, it is not so simple, especially when the company relies on many different suppliers. In such instances, you have to do some digging to find them.

Put yourself in the subject company's shoes. What type of supplies does it need for the finished product or service? As I said, you should find the answer right in the 10-K filings. If the company needs steel, it will tell you that. If it needs crude oil, it will tell you that, too. However, if you have done quite a bit of research and are still unsure, then call the company and ask them what it takes to produce what they sell. They might also tell you the specific suppliers that they use. If not, then it is your job to search for companies that provide these supplies and ask others which companies supply to your subject company.

Once you have created a list of suppliers, ask them the following questions:

How long have you been supplying to the subject company?

If the relationship between the two companies has lasted for many years, then there's a good chance that both parties are satisfied with working together. This is a good sign. As a business, you want your suppliers to be stable and reliable.

Is the subject company a big client of yours?

Big clients are important and suppliers will bend over backwards to keep those clients satisfied. Small clients are not given too much attention. If your subject company is one of the supplier's major clients, then it will have a lot more bargaining power and may receive preferential treatment. The supplier may make sure their orders are filled first, or they may ask their employees to stay late to fulfill a last-minute request.

Are you the subject company's only supplier of this particular material?

If your subject company has only one supplier, then this could be problematic if something happens to this supplier or their relationship.

If for some reason you are not able to supply your products or services, how easy would it be for a subject company to find a new supplier?

Obviously, it is best when your subject company can quickly source another supplier of equal quality. Also, it is economical when the switching costs of going from one supplier to another are low.

What kind of payment terms do you usually offer your clients?

Suppliers usually allow clients to pay for supplies 30 to 90 days after delivery. If your subject company receives better terms than the other clients, then it might be an indication that it is treated better by suppliers because of its importance. If your subject company is on COD (cash on delivery) payment terms while everybody else gets 60 days, then your company might be a bad payer. This means that the suppliers do not trust it and require cash up front. This is not good news.

Is your relationship with the subject company profitable for you?

The client and supplier relationship should be a win-win for both parties. It is not sustainable when one company is making money and the other company is barely surviving. Yes, you want your subject company to have bargaining power, but you do not want it to exploit the supplier to the point where it might go bankrupt. At the end of the day, you want a reliable source of supplies, and the only way to do it is to be fair to your suppliers by letting them earn money.

Are you able to pass your cost increases on to your clients?

If the answer is no because the supplier will lose the client, then you know that there are a lot of suppliers fighting for business. It is usually good when there is a lot of competition at the supplier level. Your subject company will most likely receive good pricing. However, if the suppliers can easily increase prices on your company, then the supplier might be in a stronger bargaining position than you would like.

For example, if CoStar is your supplier of commercial real estate information, it will raise prices on you every year and you cannot do anything about it. It is good to be CoStar and not so good to be CoStar's client. This is especially true when you are running a small appraisal office and CoStar's fees are a significant expense. You can't raise your prices for the appraisal reports but CoStar can still squeeze you year after year.

Does the subject company help you in any way to be more efficient?

In order for companies to be profitable, operations need to be efficient. This includes the supply chain, which shows up under "Cost of Goods Sold" on the income statement. Client-supplier relationships thrive when both companies work together to develop their products and services as efficiently as possible. Some clients assist their suppliers while others just bark out orders. Other times, suppliers are efficient enough that they do not need any help. It is your job to figure out what the situation is by asking questions.

What is your opinion of the subject company?

Most likely, you will get a positive response because a supplier is unlikely to say anything bad about a client that is putting food on its table. However, if you are able to find a former employee of the supplier, then you might be able to get a more honest answer.

How does the subject company compare to other competitors that you supply to?

Suppliers have intimate relationships with their clients. They see characteristics and qualities about their clients that no one else sees. Pay attention to anything they say about the competitive landscape of their clients. The hard part here is to gain their trust so that they will tell you the truth instead of painting a rosy picture. Again, asking the same question to a former employee of the supplier might give you exactly what you need.

Before you, who was supplying the subject company with the product or service that you currently supply?

The purpose of this question is simply to get the names of former suppliers who can give you information about the subject company without being afraid of losing business.

FORMER SUPPLIERS

Current suppliers know a lot about your subject company and its management, but the problem is that they are biased because they want to continue doing business with the subject company. If you can gain their trust, then they may be more forthcoming.

Former suppliers are not afraid of losing the subject company as a client because they have already stopped doing business together. If you talk to enough people, you will get some names of former suppliers.

Ask them the following questions:

What caused the relationship between you and the subject company to end?

There are all sorts of reasons why two companies may choose to stop working with each other. Maybe the subject company found a more efficient supplier or the supplier was not able to deliver. Or maybe the company decided to go in a new direction by producing a different product or service and no longer needed that supplier.

Was the relationship profitable for you?

If the relationship was not profitable for the supplier, then this is probably why the business agreement ended. However, you want to find out why it was not profitable. Was it because the supplier was not competitive, or was it because the subject company kept pushing for unrealistically low prices?

What is your opinion of the subject company?

The supplier may or may not think highly of the subject company, but either way, their answer to this question will shed light on the company's integrity and how they conduct business on a daily basis. As with former customers, they may give you a perspective that is less sugar-coated because they are no longer working with the company.

What is your opinion of their management?

You can learn eye-opening stories about the subject company's management from former suppliers. If they are angry with the management, they might tell you personal anecdotes that you would have never found out on your own without a detective.

Did the subject company always pay you on time?

If the subject company did not pay on time, then in spite of any cover story you may have heard, this may be the real reason the relationship ended. Suppliers who are paid late may experience financial difficulties. Why be involved with companies that have a history of not paying their suppliers? This may result in all kinds of lawsuits.

Did the subject company accept your prices or did it negotiate?

This will give you insight into who has more bargaining power: the client or the supplier. You might already know the answer to this question, but it is good to have it confirmed by another party.

If you had the opportunity, would you do business with the subject company again?

Obviously, you want to hear yes because this tells you that the subject company ended the relationship, not the supplier.

WANNABE SUPPLIERS

When you talk with various suppliers, you will encounter ones that are not working with the subject company. Ask them some of the same questions that you asked current and former suppliers. The most important one is to determine if they would like to supply materials to the subject company. Don't assume that they will all say yes just because suppliers are always looking for business.

Suppliers want to do business with companies that will bring them a profit. This means they want to supply their products and services to successful companies. They do not want to work with struggling clients because struggling clients pay late or not at all, cause headaches, and ask for unrealistic prices. If you consistently run into suppliers that do not want to do business with your subject company, then this is a red flag.

SUMMARY

Suppliers are an important piece of the puzzle in making your subject company's products or services successful. Because of this, they know a lot of information about their clients that can help you. When you contact them, assure them that you will not reveal the information they share with you to anyone. You want them to censor as little negative information as possible. The positive information is easy to find. The subject company's management is happy to communicate it to the world through their publications. It is the flaws and weaknesses that are hard to find.

Employees

Employees

L ike suppliers, employees are another integral part of making a product or service a success. Being inside the company every day gives employees a perspective that the management, customers, and suppliers will never see. As a scuttlebutt investor, you cannot afford to pass up the opportunity to hear what they have to say.

You can locate employees through social media sites, such as LinkedIn, where you have the capability of searching for current and past employees by the name of the company. Before contacting them directly, you can do some preliminary research online.

Glassdoor.com is a website where employees can review their companies. Because they do not have to provide their full names, they are not afraid to lose their job because of saying something negative. I always check this website to see what type of culture is present inside my subject company. Some people are very vocal on Facebook about their employers or past employers. You can check their profiles to look for clues about what it's like to be an employee of the subject company.

LinkedIn allows you to look through people's resumes. By doing so, you can get a sense of how much turnover the company is experiencing. Some industries, like retail, have lots of turnover. However, if you find a company that does not rely on low-wage workers but still has huge turnover, especially within the management, there might be something seriously wrong. How can you have a successful business when you change your personnel every few months?

Once you have created a list of current and former employees to contact, ask them the following questions:

What is it like to work for the subject company?

After you talk to several employees, you will start to get a sense of how employees feel about working for the subject company. This is especially important because employees are usually the ones who come in contact with clients.

What type of hours are employees typically required to work?

Employees that are treated like slaves are not very happy individuals. Companies should be respectful of the people who supply them with labor. While they shouldn't be given paychecks for nothing, they should be allowed to have lives outside of work. This kind of arrangement is healthy and sustainable. You can research what kinds of hours are typical for the industry and compare it to what your subject company requires.

How are people promoted?

Usually, it is preferable when your subject company promotes from within. It is better for morale, and current employees have a reason to work hard so that one day they may be promoted.

Employees hired from outside perform more poorly during their first two years on the job than do internal workers promoted into similar jobs, according to a 2011 *Administrative Science Quarterly* journal article by Matthew Bidwell. His study also showed that external hires are typically paid more and have higher exit rates. However, sometimes a company must hire outside people because they have special skills that are lacking inside the company.

How is employee performance measured?

In order for employees to receive their paychecks, they should earn them through their performance. If the subject company does not care about their employees' performance, then it might not care about other expenditures either. In this case, the shareholders should not expect great returns.

Do employees tend to stay with the company for long periods of time?

It is expensive to keep hiring and training new people. The ideal situation is when the subject company has employees that do a good job and stay with the company for long periods of time.

There are many costs that come with employee turnover. Hiring costs, severance pay, lost productivity, and lost institutional knowledge are just a few. Employees leave for many reasons such as low satisfaction with either their jobs or their employers, limited promotion and growth opportunities, or better opportunities elsewhere. Turnover costs can be surprisingly high and can vary widely from one type of position to another, as well as from one type of industry to another.

The cost of turnover can be measured as a percentage of annual wage or salary. For a nonskilled entry level worker, such as a fast-food employee, it can range from 30 to 50 percent, according to *Managing Talent Retention: An ROI Approach*, by Jack J. Phillips and Lisa Edwards. In contrast, it can range from 75 to 100 percent for a skilled hourly worker, such as a machinist, and from 200 to 400 percent for a specialist, like a computer software designer.

Turnover rates vary depending on the industry. For example, service industries have the highest rates of turnover of up to 35 percent, while the professional trade industry and the utilities industry are tied for the lowest rates of turnover at 8 percent, according to a 2011 *Society for Human Resource Management* article by Eliza Jacobs. Once the employees you interview give you a sense of what the turnover is at your subject company, you can research what the norm is for that company's industry and compare the two.

Are employees given any training?

The problem with many employers is that they want perfect employees, but they do not want to train them because it takes resources. Also, they are afraid that the employee might leave to work for a competitor soon after training. Unless the job is very low skill, the subject company should have some kind of training programs so that their employees can learn, grow, and become better at doing their jobs.

How are employees treated by the company's management?

Every company has a hierarchy. Everybody expects that. If the company's management is serious about retaining good talent, then they had better treat them with respect and dignity.

A couple of years ago, I was researching Tandy Leather, a retailer and wholesale distributor of a range of leather and leather-related products. The company looked cheap in relation to its growth rate. Also, the financials looked pristine. The company was profitable, revenues and earnings were growing, and the balance sheet was strong. In fact, it was very difficult to find anything wrong with this company.

I visited one of Tandy's retail stores and talked to an employee who was very knowledgeable about leather. What I found out was shocking. He told me a lot of changes had recently taken place within the company, most of them negative. He said that the management was so concerned with Wall Street and its stock price that they let a number of knowledgeable salespeople go and replaced them with cheaper personnel.

I realized that the perfect financial picture I had been looking at was about to change, so I immediately eliminated this company from consideration. Management that is only concerned with Wall Street and the stock price is a huge red flag for me. As I am writing this book, the stock price is down quite a bit. Sales are down and the CEO just resigned. Talking with the honest employee saved me money.

What do employees think of the upper management?

When employees have a high opinion of the top management, they are more likely to do a good job and stay with the company longer. If not, then they will always be looking for a new job, probably on the company's time.

What kind of offices do the top managers have?

There are certain businesses like law practices where having fancy offices is important because clients need to be impressed. However, for most businesses, there is no reason for lavish office suites, especially when the shareholders are paying for it. Plain vanilla offices work fine. Also, expensive tenant improvements make it harder for companies to move, allowing landlords to jack up the rental rates. Why increase your own switching costs?

Do the top managers have assigned parking spots?

Employees know that not everybody in the company is equal, but it is not necessary to rub it in their faces. This is not good for morale. However, in some businesses, reminding people of hierarchy is essential. For example, I used to work for Marcus & Millichap, a commercial real estate brokerage company. Everything was about hierarchy. The brokers that made the most money were praised and rewarded. They had their pictures put on the walls for everybody to see and admire. They were given their own offices and parking spaces. The idea was to motivate the young brokers to strive and achieve success. And it worked. In other instances, if the CEO needs to be reminded that he or she is superior, then he or she must have low self-esteem. I don't want an insecure person running my company.

What kind of car does the CEO have?

This question follows the same line of thinking. If an expensive car is required in order to impress clients and secure business deals, then it is justifiable. However, if the CEO drives a Ferrari for no other reason than to show his superiority, he is not going to be running my company. If the person is the founder of the company, then I might let it slide—the expensive car was earned.

Do the top managers ever talk to the lower-level employees and consider their suggestions?

Some managers are clueless about what their customers need or want and what it takes to satisfy them. Depending on the industry, lower-level employees may have more contact with customers than managers do, and so they may have a better sense of what they want. The best managers listen to both their clients and employees and willingly discuss solutions for challenges they face. This is what being in business is all about. If the managers of your subject company only care about what Wall Street thinks, run away.

When employees leave, do clients leave with them?

When McDonald's employees leave, the customers do not follow. They keep coming back to McDonald's no matter who serves them. However, with some businesses, clients and employees build one-on-one relationships with each other. This is the case with stockbrokers, who frequently take their clients with them when they leave to work for other companies or start their own firms. It is always better for you as an investor when your subject company is able to retain all of its clients when employees leave.

After employees leave, how easy is it to replace them?

This is a question of how highly skilled the company's employees are. Generally, the higher the skill level, the more difficult it is to find a replacement. If it is hard to find replacements, then your subject company had better be paying and treating them extra well.

SUMMARY

Employees are great source of information. Also, they are not pressured to censor information the way CEOs are, so you may be surprised how much they may be willing to tell you.

Once, I visited a company and became well acquainted with one of the employees who worked in research. I wasn't invested in the stock, but I kept my eye on it. At one point, it was so cheap that it was trading at two times earnings. I wanted so badly to back up the truck and put a lot of my money into it because it was such a no-brainer. However, before I made the purchase, I contacted that employee just to catch up. I was so glad I did because I learned that since I had visited the company, this employee had been let go because the results of research he had conducted had disappointed the management. Instead of listening to him and reporting the truth about the results to the shareholders, the company let him go and kept his findings a secret from the market. Obviously, this was a huge red flag for me, and I chose not to purchase any shares.

It is easy to find employees through LinkedIn, Facebook, the company's website, or other publicly available sources. If they are still with the company, you can call them at work. If they are former employees, then call them at their new employer.

CHAPTER 6

Competitors

Competitors

So far, you have communicated with the managers, clients, suppliers, and employees to learn about your subject company. However, if you think about it, all of these groups of people and businesses have one thing in common— they benefit from the subject company's success. Managers are rewarded with larger salaries and options. Clients benefit from great products and services. Suppliers make money from successful clients. And, employees get to have jobs and enjoy promotions from successful employers. Consequently, they might be somewhat biased. But you still need to hear what they have to say.

However, competitors have a completely different set of incentives. They hate companies that compete with them. Competitors undercut each other, steal clients from each other, and badmouth each other. More than anything, they want to crush each other. Competitors focus on the negative aspects of their adversaries, and look for weak spots where they can strike. If you want to know what is wrong with a particular company, just ask its competitors. If they trust you, they will tell you everything you need to know.

How do you locate them? Within Form 10-K, companies are required to talk about their competitive landscape, which sometimes includes listing the names of competitors. Also, you can search SEC's EDGAR (the US Securities and Exchange Commission's Electronic Data Gathering, Analysis, and Retrieval system) by specific industry. Every public company in the US has a specific industry number assigned to it called the Standard Industrial Classification (SIC) code.

With competitors, ask them some of the same questions that you asked the management. This way, you will be able to compare the answers and determine whether they are consistent. For example, if several competitors tell you that there is not much growth in the industry and that clients have low switching costs, but the CEO of your company tells you the exact opposite, then you will know that he or she is either untruthful or in complete denial. Either way, you probably want to stay away from companies like that.

The following are some questions that you should ask your competitors:

If you were a money manager and for some reason you could not buy the stock of your company, which competitor's stock would you buy?

It is most likely that the competitor would buy the stock of the strongest player. They are not going to pay attention to which player is the cheapest in relation to cash flow or which one has the best P/E ratio. They will most likely only pay attention to the business itself and how it compares to its competitors.

Which one would you short or not buy?

Here the competitor will probably name the weakest player—a company with inferior products, lousy service, and questionable management.

How do you approach research and development, and how does it to compare to your competitors?

As you know, research and development is key for many companies. It is not that easy to differentiate among the R&D departments of various competitors if you are an outsider. You need help. Talking with competitors can help you with that.

Could you describe your sales force and how it makes you competitive?

I cannot overemphasize how important it is for companies to be able to sell their products at a profit. If you have ever started a business and tried to attract clients, you know that the cost of acquiring them can literally wipe you out. Spend some time learning how various companies in the industry build their sales teams. Do they seek help from consulting firms? Do their salespeople receive any training? How do they measure marketing return on investment (ROI)?

Could you talk about various suppliers and which ones you would recommend?

The quality of any company's finished product or service is directly related to the quality of materials used. If you are a homebuilder using poor quality materials, you will build poor quality homes. If you are in the business of building starter homes, then this strategy might work, but if you are using poor quality materials to build houses for millionaires, then we have a problem. By talking with competitors, you can gain insight into the type of suppliers your subject company is using and whether it correlates with the quality that they claim their finished products have.

Would you ever hire employees away from the subject company or your other competitors?

Some companies try to steal employees away from their competitors. To do so, they may offer them higher salaries, bonus payments, or other perks. Some employees are quite valuable because of their superior training, skills, or client base. If your company's competitors show interest in poaching employees from your company, then for some reason your subject company has valuable employees. Find out why. However, if your competitor says that he or she would rather train people from scratch than lure them away from competitors, then this tells you that the competitors' employees are not very valuable.

Your margins are different from your competitors. Why?

In a competitive world, companies fight for business. As a result, the margins that they make cannot be too different from those of its competitors, especially when they sell similar products or services. It makes sense—you can't have one barber charging you $15 per haircut and another one $500 per haircut if they are practically the same. In order for such a big discrepancy to exist, there must be a reason. For example, the more expensive one could be a celebrity barber who attracts customers from all over the world. If your subject company has superior margins for no particular reason, then the competitor might shine some light as to why. Also, he or she might expose possible fraud.

Do you ever get clients who are switching from your competitors to you?

Companies that do not satisfy their customers eventually lose them. If your subject company loses customers to your competitor, then your competitor might have a better solution.

Do you ever lose clients to your competitors? Have you ever lost clients to the subject company?

Obviously, the competitor might not be willing to answer this question because it would expose its vulnerability. However, if the competitor says that he or she never loses business to your subject company, then you know that either the switching costs are too high or your company does not have a good enough solution to entice clients to switch. This is not the end of the world. You simply want to have a clear picture of where the competitors stand in comparison to each other.

SUMMARY

As you can see, you can gather valuable information about your subject company and its industry by talking with its competitors. If you never talk to the competitors, then you will be fed only positive information from the company. Nothing is only positive. We all have faults. The idea of scuttlebutt is not about finding perfect companies that are free of faults. It is about knowing what you are investing in.

CHAPTER 7

Resellers

Resellers

After businesses produce and develop their products or services, they have to sell them. They can either sell them themselves or they can sell them through third-party resellers. Think of Amazon, car dealerships, retail stores, or distributors. They are all resellers. Yes, they may be clients, but they are not end consumers.

Manufacturers often have an emotional attachment to their products. It is understandable because they are heavily invested in what they make. They produced it from scratch, so it is their baby. Not only might they be biased, they may also be delusional about them. Resellers do not fall in love with their products the way manufacturers sometimes do; they fall in love with the products that make them money. They are interested in carrying products that they can move. In my experience researching companies, I have found that resellers will even tell you which products are actually selling.

Once, when I was at a restaurant in Nashville, I had a waiter who was in the habit of paying attention to which menu items were left unfinished at the end of each meal. Based on that, he was able to point out which items were well liked and which to avoid. Unfortunately, the owner of the restaurant wouldn't listen to his feedback and insisted on leaving the unpopular items on the menu. In this case, the waiter was like the reseller and the owner was like the manufacturer.

These are some questions you want to ask resellers:

- *Which products in this category are popular and why?*
- *What do you think of the subject company's products?*
- *Do they sell out?*
- *Why do people buy them?*
- *Why do people buy the competitors' products?*
- *When you sell out, does the subject company respond quickly to refill your orders?*
- *Is the subject company responsive to your feedback about their products or services?*
- *Does the product or service experience lots of returns?*

I surveyed a number of resellers when I was researching a company called Arctic Cat. At the end of 2009, Arctic Cat, which is a manufacturer and seller of snowmobiles and ATVs, was trading for half of its inventory. In other words, the stock was extremely cheap. But I had never heard of it before and wanted to find out the strength of the brand. I called approximately 100 dealerships that sold Arctic Cat's products and learned that not only was Arctic Cat a serious snowmobile brand, but that many customers favored it over its competitors. Based on this information combined with my other research, I felt comfortable purchasing the stock, which, by the way, turned out to be a huge winner.

If your company's product is sold on Amazon, you can take a different approach. As you know, Amazon sells all kinds of products from books to electronics. Check if the company's products are sold on Amazon and read the reviews. Also, pay attention to the total number of reviews, which may be an indication of how well the product is selling. For example, look at the number of reviews on these two books.

The Little Book That Still Beats the Market Sep 7, 2010
by Joel Greenblatt and Andrew Tobias

Hardcover
$13.73 $24.95 √Prime
Get it by Tomorrow, Jul 12

More Buying Choices
$9.99 used & new (86 offers)

Kindle Edition
$10.99
Auto-delivered wirelessly

☆☆☆☆☆ ▾ 401

#1 Best Seller in Commodities Trading

FREE Shipping on orders over $35

Why Are We So Clueless about the Stock Market?
how to... Sep 1, 2009
by Mariusz Skonieczny

Paperback
$14.83 $14.95 √Prime

More Buying Choices
$12.00 used & new (38 offers)

Kindle Edition
$9.99
Auto-delivered wirelessly

☆☆☆☆☆ ▾ 38

Trade-in yours for an Amazon Gift Card up to $4.40
FREE Shipping on orders over $35

The Little Book That Still Beats the Market was written by Joel Greenblatt and has 401 reviews. *Why Are We So Clueless about the Stock Market?* was written by me and has only 38 reviews. Which one do you think sells more copies? It is obvious that his book outsells mine any day of the week.

You can make the same comparisons with other products sold on Amazon. Of course, the problem is that not all companies sell their products on Amazon, but if they do, you had better read the reviews and compare them to the competing products.

SUMMARY

Resellers know what products move. They know what people like. In some instances, they understand the end customer better than the manufacturers do. Also, they are not as emotionally tied to their products, especially when they carry different brands. So, talk to them. Learn from their insights.

CHAPTER 8

Installers and Servicers

Installers and Servicers

S ome products need to be installed or serviced after they are sold. For example, automobiles need frequent servicing and repair. Heating and air conditioning products need to be installed and then maintained and serviced. Software needs to be installed, updated, and reprogrammed, meaning replaced with new software. These are called aftermarket industries. You can learn a great deal about a company's products and services by interviewing individuals and businesses that are involved in related servicing, repair, and installation activities.

I live near Elkhart, Indiana, the RV capital of the world. When I hear that someone works in Elkhart, I automatically assume that they work in the RV industry. My neighbor repairs and services RVs made by various manufacturers such as Winnebago, Thor Industries, and Country Coach. When I spoke with him at a cookout, I was able to learn which manufacturers produce quality RVs and which ones cut corners. He said, "It is amazing that people will spend $500,000 on a piece of junk."

Do you think I would have learned this by reading 10-K filings and browsing the manufacturer's website? Not a chance. Every manufacturer is a leading company in its own view. Scuttlebutt is the only way you can learn the truth.

When you are studying a subject company, make a list of companies involved in the aftermarket. This could include auto mechanics, home remodelers, or HVAC repair technicians. Obviously, your list will be dependent on the type of product or service your company makes or provides.

Ask them the following questions:

- *Which brands break the most?*
- *Which brands last the longest?*
- *What has been your experience with the subject company's products?*
- *How do these products compare to competing products?*
- *Are people happy after they purchase the subject company's products?*
- *Have you noticed any changes in the quality of the subject company's products over the last several years?*
- *Is the manufacturing company responsive to feedback from professionals like yourself?*

SUMMARY

I guarantee you that 99.9 percent of investors have never talked to people who repair and service the products of the companies in which they buy stock. They would rather listen to Wall Street for stock recommendations. But Wall Street analysts don't do their homework either. Scuttlebutt research is not rocket science, but it does take work. What is frustrating is that you might know more than anyone else about the company, but you may still not get rewarded because everybody else that trades the stock lacks the information that you have. With that being said, I would still rather know than not know.

CHAPTER 9

Board of Directors

Board of Directors

The board of directors of a public company is elected to represent the shareholders. Its members are supposed to provide advice to the company and make sure that the managers are doing what is best for shareholders. Interviewing a few members of the board can really give you insight into how the company is truly managed versus how it appears on paper to be managed.

The names of the members of the board are listed in the proxy statement. Create a list of current and former board members. You will need to look at proxy statements from prior years to find the names of former board members.

The following are questions for the current board members:

What is your role? What value do you bring to the table?

Board members are paid money to serve their companies. They should have something to offer, otherwise, how can they advise the CEO? If you cannot figure out the value of the board member to the company, then he or she might only be there as a "yes man" to the CEO.

What are you currently doing professionally?

Carl Icahn has said that one of the problems with many boards of directors is that the board members rely on the income from the companies they serve. Consequently, if they rock the boat too much, they will lose that income. For them to be effective, they need to have other sources of income.

How much time do you dedicate to the company?

If they spend barely any time serving the company, then it is unlikely they will admit it, but you can still make them explain what they do to earn their fees.

How did you become a board member?

Figure out whether they were selected by the CEO, recommended by a large shareholder (the preferred method), or introduced to the company by another board member. Why was this person chosen to serve?

Can you talk about your business successes and failures?

Ideally, you want to see board members with extensive business experience and a track record of success. However, you and I both know that many successful people failed before achieving success. If the board member cannot tell you anything about past failures, then either he or she is not being forthcoming with you, or he or she is not qualified to be on the board.

What value do the other board members bring to the table?

Every board member should be on the board of directors for a reason. The members should know the value that the other members bring to the table.

Why did so and so leave the board of directors?

The compositions of boards of directors change all the time. However, sometimes the changes happen because of disagreements. Try to see if you can learn about the reasons behind resignations. Was it because the member could not agree with the management or other members? Most of the time, board members will be cautious about what they say, but after they warm up to you, they might give you some useful clues about the truth.

I see that you serve on a particular committee. Could you describe your responsibilities as a committee member?

Boards of directors have committees, such as the compensation committee and the audit committee. Let the person articulate to you what his or her responsibilities are on those committees.

Here are some questions to ask former board members:

- *Why did you leave?*
- *Did the board members work well together?*
- *What is your opinion of the current CEO?*
- *Do the current board members add any value to the company or are they just "yes men?"*

SUMMARY

Interviewing the current and former board members can give you more insight into the company. There will be many times that these individuals will be cautious about what they tell you. You can't blame them. They don't know you. But if you are good at putting people at ease, then they might open up. A lot of times what I do is I offer them something. For example, I might write an analysis on the company and offer to send it to them. Then, when I call them, they will already be familiar with who I am. If the article is positive, then they know I am on their side.

One time, I wrote a negative article about the competitor of a particular company, and three of that company's board members contacted me. So, of course, I took this opportunity to connect with them. I learned so much that I doubled my knowledge of the company by talking with them. I always ask if we can chat on the phone.

CHAPTER 10

Shareholders

Shareholders

The Internet has made it very easy for shareholders of various companies to communicate with each other. Every publicly traded company has some shareholders who are extremely well informed and other shareholders who know very little. As a scuttlebutt investor, you can identify the knowledgeable ones to help you increase your understanding. Here is how to locate them.

- Proxy statement
- 13-D and 13-G filings
- Message boards
- StockTwits and Twitter
- Investment-sharing websites
- Blogs
- Shareholder meetings

PROXY STATEMENT

Every year, publicly traded companies are required to provide investors with a proxy statement explaining matters that require a vote by the shareholders. This statement lists shareholders that own more than five percent of the shares.

SCHEDULE 13-D AND 13-G FILINGS

Shareholders that accumulate more than five percent of a company's shares must file either Schedule 13-D or 13-G with the SEC. You can access SEC's EDGAR and search for these filings.

MESSAGE BOARDS

To discuss various companies, investors go on message boards such as Yahoo Finance, InvestorsHub, or Stockhouse (mainly for Canadian stocks). Out of all the comments, some will be intelligent ones from knowledgeable investors. You should try to connect with them. I have developed many relationships through message boards. At first, I e-mail them through the message board, and then I try to chat with them on the phone or Skype.

STOCKTWITS AND TWITTER

People use StockTwits and Twitter to share investment ideas with each other. Search for discussion about your subject company and connect with the individuals that seem well informed.

INVESTMENT-SHARING WEBSITES

Websites such as Value Investors Club, SumZero, Distressed Debt Investing, and MicroCapClub are places where investors share investment ideas with each other. Finding a write-up of a company you are researching is an opportunity to connect with the author of that write-up, who is likely also invested in that company.

BLOGS

During your due diligence research, you may come across a variety of blogs written by investors who follow your company. These blogs may be written by individuals who discuss their personal investments, or they may be written by employees of hedge funds who are sharing investment ideas from their employer as part of their job. Either way, you can connect with the author, if you think it would be helpful, or with investors who write comments on the article.

Also, you can start your own blog and write about your investment ideas. By doing this, shareholders will come to you instead of you having to search for them. I do a combination of both.

In 2009, I wrote a report about Dover Motorsports, which is a promoter of two NASCAR racing events. The whole thesis behind the report was that the company was going to sell its two NASCAR events to one of two major competitors. In the past, one NASCAR event had sold for as much as $100 million. Dover Motorsports had a market cap of $80 million, which I thought was extremely low considering that the company owned two NASCAR events. After I published the report on Seeking Alpha, I was contacted by Mario Cibelli, the managing member of Marathon Partners. His company was a major shareholder that had launched an activist campaign against the company to force the sale. I met with him and learned that despite claims made otherwise, Dover Motorsports' management was not at all interested in maximizing shareholder value. They were unlikely to sell the NASCAR assets because the personal status they provided was worth much more to them than making money for shareholders. Soon after that, I sold my shares and moved on. It is now seven years later and the company still has the same market cap and the assets still have not been sold.

SHAREHOLDER MEETINGS

Every year, public companies hold shareholder meetings. This is one of the best places to get to know serious investors in particular companies. If they make the effort to come to shareholder meetings, then this means that they follow these companies closely.

Here are some questions that you can ask fellow shareholders:

How long have you been involved with the company?

As you would expect, long-term shareholders usually have more knowledge about the company simply because they have been following the story for so long. Also, they went through the ups and downs, so they are more useful to you than someone who just bought the stock a week ago.

How did you learn about this company?

This question can help you separate the knowledgeable investors from the rest. If the person heard about the company because he or she is a supplier or a friend of the CEO, then you know that this is not an ordinary shareholder.

Why are you invested in the company?

By asking this question, you are trying to see if other investors have chosen this company for the same reasons you have. Maybe there are other reasons that you never considered.

What is your opinion of the management?

You already formed your own opinion of the management. But another shareholder might tell you that the management is great while you think to yourself that you couldn't disagree more. Regardless, it's helpful to learn what others think, especially if they have a different opinion. They may know something you don't.

Obviously, there are a lot more questions that you can ask other shareholders about the company. The more you know yourself, the better and more detailed your questions will be. Note that this time, you should not only receive information but also offer information because other shareholders that you speak with should feel that being in contact with you is also beneficial to them. If you do your homework, then sharing information with them should not be an issue. Of course, you should remember that some of your sources provided information to you trusting that you would not repeat it, so use discretion when deciding what to share.

You can also contact former shareholders, especially ones who were long-term shareholders. To locate them, look through old proxy statements. Learn from them why they sold. If the stock price increased during their holding period, then they probably just took profits. But if this was not the case, then they may have sold because they found something better to invest in or something happened that disappointed them. If it's the latter, find out what it was.

The reason could be as simple as a loss of patience, but it could also be something serious like catching the CEO in a lie. This happened to me once. I had been talking about once a month to the CEO of a particular company in which I was invested. Because I always took notes, I was able to tell when he blatantly lied to me. I sold the stock immediately and decided never to invest in it again. I do not do business with crooks and liars. This incident made me realize that shareholders would never do well with this guy at the helm.

SUMMARY

The purpose of connecting with other investors is to share knowledge about particular companies. If you build relationships with them and stay in touch, the lines of communication can stay open for many years. As new developments happen within the company, you will likely receive updated communications. This is good because it takes time to truly understand a company. You gather one piece here, one there, and soon, you start to form a picture.

CHAPTER 11

Analysts

Analysts

There are two types of analysts: sell side and buy side. The sell-side analysts work for the Wall Street firms, and the buy-side analysts work for the buyers, who are usually hedge funds or mutual funds. When you contact the larger shareholders of your subject company, you will likely have to talk to buy-side analysts if the shareholder is big enough to hire them. In this section, when I say analysts, I am referring to the sell-side analysts.

Sell-side analysts cover a list of companies, usually in specific industries. They are supposed to know their companies inside and out, which includes doing scuttlebutt research. Obviously, you can benefit tremendously by interviewing them about your companies. But here is the problem.

They provide their research to the clients of their firms. If you are not a client, then they are unlikely to help you unless, of course, you have a personal relationship with them. Their job is to convince institutional investors to conduct their trading through their employers. To achieve that, they need to make themselves valuable, which means providing proprietary information and arranging meetings with management.

This is a Catch-22. If they write negative reports about the companies that they cover, the companies will cut off their access to the management and they won't be able to arrange one-on-one meetings between their institutional clients and the management. So, they rarely write negative reports. This makes them useless. They exchange real information when they speak with the institutional investors privately on the phone or at lunch. But if you are not an institutional investor, you are never going to get anything useful out of them.

I almost never talk to analysts for two reasons. One is what I just described. The second is that the kind of companies I invest in barely have any analyst coverage. I mainly invest in small and microcap stocks because I feel that I can get an edge by doing my own scuttlebutt research. What advantage can I get by using the scuttlebutt method on a company that is covered by lots of analysts?

SUMMARY

If you can get useful information out of analysts, then go for it. However, a lot of the time, investors make the mistake of thinking that analysts will be helpful and that they are there for the good of the investment community. You should keep in mind that they have no responsibility to you. They don't work for you. Sell-side analysts work for brokerage firms. Brokerage firms work for publicly traded companies. Publicly traded companies hire Wall Street firms because they want to raise money by selling shares to investors. Consequently, analysts are nothing but glorified cheerleaders there to help the publicly traded companies sell stock. In order to do this, they write and distribute reports about these companies. So, when they are nice to you and have great things to say about the company, they are simply trying to unload shares. I'm not saying you should not listen to them, but you should know what their incentives are. In my opinion, it is better to do your own work and not rely on anyone else to do it for you.

CHAPTER 12

Original Researchers

Original Researchers

Depending on the type of business they are in, some companies must keep improving and creating new products in order to stay relevant. Consequently, for those companies, research and development, whether done in-house or provided by an outside company or research university, is not optional, it is required.

To determine how new technology under development can impact a company's future revenues, contact the original researchers. I can guarantee you that most will be shocked that an investor is contacting them, and will appreciate someone noticing their work and acknowledging their expertise. They can provide you with various reports about their findings and can give you background information about why they decided to take their research in a certain direction. They may even be able to give you a sense of how big the market is for the particular product.

In 2013, I was researching Image Sensing Systems, which is a company that provides products and solutions to optimize traffic flow, enhance driver safety, regulate air quality, and address security and surveillance concerns. I was particularly interested in the company because of a special video detection product that it made called Autoscope. You have probably seen Autoscope cameras on the top of traffic lights.

They use machine vision technology, which uses image-based camera sensors in order to detect vehicles in real time. This allows traffic lights to be changed according to traffic patterns. Without devices like this, you would have to sit at red lights even if there were no cars on the other side. Autoscope uses a technology that competes with the traditional method of controlling stoplights through in-ground sensors.

The technology behind Autoscope cameras was originally developed at the University of Minnesota under the direction of the company's founder, Dr. Panos G. Michalopoulos who was a director of the company. To learn about the technology, I contacted him and he told me quite a bit about his invention. His comments gave me a better idea of how hard it would be for competitors to copy it and use it in their own devices. I came away from the conversation with a much better sense of whether I wanted to invest in the company.

SUMMARY

Don't just let the management sell you on the hype of what the future can be. CEOs can be great salespeople. This is one of their jobs. But this doesn't mean that you can't do some digging on your own. Talking with the original researchers can help. Think about it. If you developed something from scratch, don't you think you would have some kind of opinion about how successful you think it can become? You might not be right, but you definitely have more insight than someone with no clue.

CHAPTER 13

Former Management

Former Management

Former managers are no longer with the company, so they do not have to be cheerleaders anymore. Consequently, they can shine some light on the good and the bad of the subject company. To locate their names, look through old 10-K filings or proxy statements. Then, you will need to do some research to find their new contact information.

When you have compiled a list of former members of the management team, ask them the following questions:

Why did you leave?

When managers leave, companies devise cover-up reasons so as not to scare the market. Now that they are no longer with the company, they may reveal the true reasons for leaving. It could be as simple as retirement, but it could also be an internal struggle with major shareholders, other members of the management team, or the board of directors.

Was it difficult to work with the board?

The board of directors is supposed to represent the investors. If the board ousted the management, then maybe they truly are representing investors. However, maybe the board was easy to work with and the manager you are interviewing left for another reason.

How did the shareholders treat you?

Big shareholders can get pushy and they have the right to do so. They own the company. However, sometimes they are wrong. Sometimes, they are just people who sit in front of their computers all day thinking that they can run the companies better than the CEOs. I have seen many companies fail after shareholders took over. Listen to what the former managers have to say about the shareholders. Whether you agree or not is unimportant. Every conflict has three sides to the story.

Do you think that the company will succeed with the current management in place?

If the former managers think that the current management will succeed, then this is fantastic. If they don't, then it would be nice to hear their argument.

One of the companies that I own hired a new CEO, and because I follow my companies pretty closely, I had gotten to know the former CEO fairly well. When he was let go, I wanted to know what had happened, and I also wanted to hear his thoughts about the new CEO, who had already been involved with the company as a major shareholder prior to becoming CEO. After calling the former CEO, I learned that he and the new CEO did not get along. He told me, "We disagree on the strategy, but he is a worker. He gets stuff done. I give him that." Positive feedback about the new CEO from someone who didn't actually like him was particularly interesting to me. When I talked with major shareholders who knew the new CEO personally, they echoed the same sentiments. I learned that he is not only hardworking, but obsessed with his work. One of them told me, "He lives and breathes this business. He has no family—maybe an occasional girlfriend. If you took this business from him, I think he would die." He is not a promoter. He is simply a doer. This is exactly the kind of person that I want in charge of my company—someone committed to making the company a success. I would have never learned this about him without scuttlebutt research.

SUMMARY

People tend to forget about the former managers. You shouldn't. They know a lot. They could save you a lot of money by pointing out problems that you would not have noticed otherwise. You never know what you are going to learn until you interview them.

CHAPTER 14

Conclusion

Conclusion

In this book, Scuttlebutt research is one of the best ways to learn about companies. One of the most important benefits of scuttlebutt is that it can give you conviction. In the movie *The Big Short*, an adaptation of Michael Lewis's book by the same name, the character Mark Baum, based on real-life investor Steve Eisman, and his team used scuttlebutt methods to confirm their suspicions that the housing market had overheated and was about to crash.

They did something few investors did at that time—visit an area with one of the highest ratios of median home prices to income in the United States—Miami. Walking around one of the new subdivisions that had been virtually abandoned, they sensed firsthand the desolation and despair of the residents, or former residents. While the prevailing narrative was that the housing market was still hot, they saw vacant houses for sale, unfinished houses where construction had stopped, and a number of vacant lots with curbs, gutters, and streetlights installed—evidence that the developer had jumped the gun.

Their quest also involved talking to a local real estate agent, mortgage brokers, a CDO (collateralized debt obligation) manager, an employee of the ratings agency Standard & Poor's, and a renter whose landlord was 90 days delinquent on his mortgage. They learned that the real estate agent had sold a particular house four times for a higher price each time and the current owners were willing to sell for the same price they paid, a sign that prices had peaked. The mortgage brokers were writing four to six times more loans than they had been before the housing boom, and the bonuses they were paid on subprime adjustable-rate loans were five times what they were paid on fixed-rate prime loans. The CDO manager admitted he didn't care about the risk he was exposing investors to, and Standard & Poor's was scared clients would go to Moody's if they didn't give them favorable ratings. And, as if they needed any more confirmation of the bizarro nature of the times, the landlord had put the mortgage in his dog's name.

It seemed that everyone around them thought the housing market was still hot, and they had been afraid they were missing something. Their research showed them they hadn't.

Not very many investors attempt scuttlebutt because it is easier to passively listen to Wall Street and the companies themselves. However, if you want to gain an informational edge over other investors, you must do the work.

With that being said, the scuttlebutt method is most effective with small- or medium-sized companies where analyst coverage is limited. You can easily become one of the most knowledgeable investors in these companies. Also, when you are dealing with small cap or microcap companies, you might become a victim of fraud. This is why so many investors shy away from small companies. However, if you use the scuttlebutt approach, you can check whether the company has real customers or suppliers because you will talk with them. If Wall Street did this kind of work, then WorldCom or Enron would have never happened.

You should also understand that scuttlebutt research is not something that you do just one time. Yes, you should do it before you buy a stock, but when you own the stock of a company, you should continuously be in touch with various people connected to the company. Circumstances change. Companies are like living organisms. By continuously exercising scuttlebutt methods, you will have your finger on the company's pulse at all times.

Other Books by this Author

Other Books by
this Author

The following is a list of other books written by Mariusz Skonieczny:

- *Why Are We So Clueless about the Stock Market?*
- *The Basics of Understanding Financial Statements*
- *100 Ways to Find Investment Ideas*
- *Gold Production from Beginning to End*
- *Due Diligence: How to Research a Stock*
- *Investment Wisdom*

Works Cited

Works Cited

Banjo, Shelly. "Here's the Report that May Have Prompted the Lumber Liquidators Raid." *The Wall Street Journal*. Dow Jones & Company, Inc., 9 October 2013. Web. 4 June 2016.

Bidwell, Matthew. "Paying More to Get Less: The Effects of External Hiring versus Internal Mobility." *Administrative Science Quarterly* 56.3 (2011): 369-407. Web. 4 June 2016.

California. California Environmental Protection Agency. *Lumber Liquidators Pays $2.5 Million to Settle California Clean Air Claims*. Sacramento: California Environmental Protection Agency, 22 March 2016. Web. 5 June 2016.

Chen, Q., Guo, X., Ji, F., Wang, J., Wang, J., and Cao, P. "Warping and Surface Checking Analysis of Engineered Wood Flooring for Heating Systems." *BioResources* 10.3 (2015): 1. Web. 4 June 2016.

Cooper, Anderson. "Lumber Liquidators Linked to Health and Safety Violations." *CBS*. CBS Interactive, Inc., 1 March 2015. Web. 4 June 2016.

Farris, Paul W., et al. *Marketing Metrics: The Definitive Guide to Measuring Marketing Performance*. Upper Saddle River: Pearson Education, Inc., 2010. Print.

Fisher, Philip A. *Common Stocks and Uncommon Profits*. Hoboken: John Wiley & Sons, Inc., 1996, 2003. Print.

"IARC Classifies Formaldehyde as Carcinogenic to Humans." *International Agency for Research on Cancer*. World Health Organization, International Agency for Research on Cancer, 15 June 2004. Web. 4 June 2016.

Jacobs, Eliza. "Executive Brief: Differences in Employee Turnover Across Key Industries." *Society for Human Resource Management*. SHRM, December 2011. Web. 23 June 2016.

Lewis, Michael. *The Big Short: Inside the Doomsday Machine*. New York: W. W. Norton & Company, Inc., 2010. Print.

Liquidating the Forests: Hardwood Flooring, Organized Crime, and the World's Last Siberian Tigers. Washington: Environmental Investigation Agency, 2013. Web. 4 June 2016.

Lowe's Companies, Inc. *2007 Annual Report, Form 10-K*. Mooresville, NC: Lowe's Companies, Inc., 2008. Web.

Lowe's Companies, Inc. *2010 Annual Report, Form 10-K*. Mooresville, NC: Lowe's Companies, Inc., 2011. Web.

Lowe's Companies, Inc. *2012 Annual Report, Form 10-K*. Mooresville, NC: Lowe's Companies, Inc., 2013. Web.

Lowe's Companies, Inc. *2015 Annual Report, Form 10-K*. Mooresville, NC: Lowe's Companies, Inc., 2016. Web.

Lumber Liquidators, Inc. *2007 Form 10-K*. Toano, VA: Lumber Liquidators, Inc., 2008. Web.

Lumber Liquidators, Inc. *2010 Form 10-K*. Toano, VA: Lumber Liquidators, Inc., 2011. Web.

Lumber Liquidators, Inc. *2015 Form 10-K*. Toano, VA: Lumber Liquidators, Inc., 2016. Web.

Lumber Liquidators, Inc. *Form S-1, Registration Statement.* Toano, VA: Lumber Liquidators, Inc., 2007. Web.

Lumber Liquidators, Inc.. *Lumber Liquidators Announces Second Quarter 2012 Financial Results and Raises Full Year Outlook.* Toano: Lumber Liquidators, 25 July 2012. Web. 2 June 2016.

Monfort, Ashley. "Homeland Security Searches Lumber Liquidators in Henrico, Toano." *WWBT NBC12*, Frankly and Raycom Media, 26 September 2013. Web. 2 June 2016.

Phillips, Jack J., and Lisa Edwards. *Managing Talent Retention: An ROI Approach.* San Francisco: Pfeiffer, by John Wiley & Sons, Inc., 2009. Print.

"Russian Far East: Hardwood Flooring, Organized Crime, and the World's Last Siberian Tigers." *Environmental Investigation Agency.* Environmental Investigation Agency, n.d. Web. 4 June 2016.

The Big Short. Director Adam McKay. Performers Christian Bale, Steve Carell, Ryan Gosling, and Brad Pitt. Paramount Pictures, 2015. Film.

The Home Depot, Inc. *Fiscal Year 2010 Form 10-K.* Atlanta, GA: The Home Depot, Inc., 2011. Web.

The Home Depot, Inc. *Fiscal Year 2015 Form 10-K.* Atlanta, GA: The Home Depot, Inc., 2016. Web.

United States. Agency for Toxic Substances and Disease Registry. *Addendum to the Toxicological Profile for Formaldehyde.* Atlanta: US Department of Health and Human Services, October 2010. Web. 4 June 2016.

United States. Agency for Toxic Substances and Disease Registry. *Possible Health Implications from Exposure to Formaldehyde Emitted from Laminate Flooring Samples Tested by the Consumer Product Safety Commission.* Atlanta: US Department of Health and Human Services, 22 March 2016. Web. 4 June 2016.

United States. Agency for Toxic Substances and Disease Registry. *Public Health Statement: Formaldehyde, CAS# 50-00-0.* Atlanta: US Department of Health and Human Services, September 2008. Web. 5 June 2016.

United States. Agency for Toxic Substances and Disease Registry. *Toxicological Profile for Formaldehyde.* Atlanta: US Department of Health and Human Services, July 1999. Web. 5 June 2016.

United States. Department of Justice. *Lumber Liquidators Inc. Pleads Guilty to Environmental Crimes and Agrees to Pay More than $13 Million in Fines, Forfeiture and Community Service Payments.* Washington: US Department of Justice, 22 October 2015. Web. 5 June 2016.

United States. Department of Justice. *Lumber Liquidators Inc. Sentenced for Illegal Importation of Hardwood and Related Environmental Crimes: Virginia Hardwood Flooring Company to Pay $13 Million, Largest Lacey Act Penalty Ever.* Washington: US Department of Justice, 1 February 2016. Web. 4 June 2016.

United States. Judicial Panel on Multidistrict Litigation. *In Re: Lumber Liquidators Chinese-Manufactured Flooring Products Marketing, Sales Practices and Products Liability Litigation.* Washington: US Judicial Panel on Multidistrict Litigation, 12 June 2015. Web. 5 June 2016.

United States of America v. Lumber Liquidators, Inc. Criminal No. 2:15cr126, United States District Court for the Eastern District of Virginia. 22 October 2015. Web. 5 June 2016.

"Update 2–Lumber Liquidators Cooperating in Wood Imports Probe." *Reuters.* Thomson Reuters, 27 September 2013. Web. 2 June 2016.

Wallace, Gregory. "Stock Tumbles After Raid of Lumber Liquidators." *CNN Money.* Cable News Network, A Time Warner Company, 27 September 2013. Web. 2 June 2016.

Zhou, Xuhua. "Illegal Products Could Spell Big Trouble at Lumber Liquidators." *Seeking Alpha.* Seeking Alpha, 20 June 2013. Web. 2 June 2016.

www.ingramcontent.com/pod-product-compliance
Lightning Source LLC
Chambersburg PA
CBHW071855200326
41519CB00016B/4388